TIM THC

DISCOVER THE POWER WITHIN TO TRANSFORM YOUR OUTSIDE WORLD.

© 2019 Tim Thomas

First published 2019

ISBN (paperback): 978-0-6484604-2-8
 ISBN (eBook): 978-0-6484604-3-5
Published by Tim Thomas

w I www.breathworkinbed.com.au

e I info@breathworkinbed.com.au

Cover design: Amy-Lee Farr - www.amyleefarr.com
Cover image of Tim Thomas - www.eventphotos.com.au

Book design: Gordon Thompson

What if **something already** inside of you could change everything outside of you?

That **something** was discovered, by an Australian Special Forces Soldier, with 5 minutes left to live …

Tim Thomas, born in June 1973, father of two. After losing his job in 2003, Tim became the oldest 'recruit' in the Australian Defence Force DRSF scheme (Direct Recruiting into Special Forces). This scheme took appropriately screened civilians into the mysterious world of Special Forces.

Having served his country in Afghanistan and East Timor as a Commando, Tim left the Army in 2010.

Tim is also dyslexic. Tim's dyslexia gives him a unique insight into everyday experiences. For the past 8 years Tim has worked very hard in the veteran recover space, helping other veterans on their journey of healing post-service.

CONTENTS

ACKNOWLEDGEMENTS

The back cover photograph is used with kind permission of Greenslopes Private Hospital and the image was made by www.eventphotos.com.au. The photograph on page 143 is used with the kind permission of Gallipoli Medical Research Foundation.

Thanks to Andrew Farrell at eBook Alchemy and Gordon Thompson of Clouds of Magellan Press for production services. Also, to the many people who helped in my journey of healing and recovery post-service. You know who you are. Without your help this book could not have been written. For that you have my eternal Gratitude.

AUTHOR'S NOTE

This book is a reprint. A 'pivot point' in my life occurred since first publication in 2019. The word ENERGY is used a lot in this book. However, I invite the reader to occasionally try replacing the word ENERGY, with the word BREATH.

Everything started changing for me the moment I could create/control more energy. It allowed me to take actions & think from a higher perspective. This book was written to share these insights. However, looking back on it, the precursor for all of my powerful insights/change (where it all began) was with simple **breathwork.** This reprinted version intends to add to the mental insights from the original. I seek to highlight the role of physical practices (like breathwork). For additional breathwork resources,

Please use the Breathwork in bed app or visit

www.breathworkinbed.com.au

Being dyslexic, I have struggled to read all my life; However, my body has always had a sense of 'knowing' what feels right. I knew that my eyes got lost when looking at a page of uniform print.

As a result, this book has been structured for 'ease of access' (especially for the non-reading types like myself).

Bold words and centered lines allow the eye to 'lock onto' and hold the page structure.

I believe we should do everything we can to make empowering information (both mental & physical) accessible to those who need it. Sincerely, Tim Thomas

INTRODUCTION

What if there was **something** inside of you, that could change everything outside of you?

It could have been the gravity of my own impending death in Afghanistan, but before I discovered 'That something,' my body and mind were shutting down.

I've since found that what I discovered has gone by a lot of different names throughout the centuries.

For myself, I simply call it **energy**.

Energy is real. It's valuable, and it's already **inside you**.

Don't think 'Energy' like it's mystical; I have a faith, but this feels different. This feels more like discovering a hidden human super power; **Real** power and influence over any situation.

Let's begin the journey!

1

ENERGY BASICS

'ENERGY can grow anything you want'
Tim Thomas

To understand energy, you first need to understand there are two VERY different types of people in this world,

and they're both YOU...
True Story!
Allow me to explain.

Have you ever wondered why some days life is great, and everything is going your way? The kind of day that hours seem like seconds. Whilst on other days, life's a struggle. Even small things seem hard. Seconds seem like hours. Thoughts of 'Why am I doing this? Seriously?? Urg, don't talk to me till I've had a coffee!'

This is more common than you think.

Simply put, the difference between good and bad days is the amount of ENERGY we have in **our system**.

ENERGY is real. It's valuable, and it's already inside you.

Energy can be increased or decreased depending on our **choices**.

More Energy = More options and more hope.
Less Energy = Less options and no hope of change.

Consciously or not, it's been happening your whole life … really, really.

Learn to manage it **right**, and it can solve any problem & change ANY situation.

This book will show you how to create real, feel good **energy**! (more powerful and permanent than coffee or Red Bull.)

The best example of this **real** energy in action is an experience I mentioned in the Foreword.

Getting shot at and rocketed was very common in Afghanistan. We'd already lost men and had limbs blown off others.

Death was no stranger.

I'd actually made my peace with it. I got some real good life insurance and made my **final** video messages to my children, family and friends.

This may sound brutal, but I did believe in old fashioned service to my country. I couldn't let it be 'someone else's' father, husband or son. I was also a working-class man with no higher education. At that time, (before my higher thinking kicked in) risking my life was **all I had** to earn above minimum wage and give my family the life I wanted them to have.

Afghanistan 2009. Author en-route to enemy engagement with mounted 50 Cal machine gun. A picture says a thousand words …

However, this ambush had an **annoying** twist on death … (like death needed it.) See, tactically, the rear vehicle of the convoy is **least defended**. As a result, it's the rear vehicle that generally gets **attacked**. As a result, the order came down to put all the heavily armoured vehicles, called 'Bush Masters' (that RPGs – Rocket-Propelled Grenades – couldn't penetrate) to **the rear** of the convoy. Our vehicle had no armour. It was simply a 4WD with the roof cut off. This was very standard for Australian Special Forces. However, in the confusion, a Bush Master pushed into the convoy ahead of us, **cutting us off. We** were now the **rear vehicle** in the convoy.

SH*T!

Everyone in that vehicle knew what was going to happen next.

My vehicle commander said (as he actioned up his machine gun), 'Fella's, if this goes the way I think it will; It's been a pleasure serving with you.'

It's funny, but in moments like that you notice the small things … Like hearing your own 'Dinky Di' Australian accent spoken back to you; but this was not a movie, and we didn't have a pause button …

I knew I was going to die, and **soon** …

I had a wife and two young kids back in Australia.
Now, if you think of your life up until this point; There are probably large portions of it dedicated to pursuing what you thought at the time were **very** important agendas. They could be School grades, career choices, work priorities, making money etc.

Now, I'm not a highly educated man, but I discovered something **powerful**; Death sorts out what is really important to you, **really** quickly. In Afghanistan with less than 5 minutes left to live, I discovered something about myself …
JUST HOW PISSED OFF I COULD GET!!

We're all about to **die** because THAT F**KING AS**LE CUT US OFF!! (It's funny when I look back on my own reactions. I hope you see the humour in this also.) I thought, 'They're going to return our flag-covered bodies to Australia. They're going to carry us down the ramp of the aeroplane with all this BULLS**T ceremony, all because some ASS**LE Bush Master driver, cut us off!!'

So what does this have to do with ENERGY?

Energy not properly managed creates **fear**.

You'd think that as a soldier I'd get used to fear. Fact was I never did, but there's something helpful about being exposed to fear so often. You do get a very clear understanding of how   fear   actually works,   and   it's fascinating!
I found that Fear has a goal, and it's not to scare you.

Fear's ultimate goal is to immobilise you. To stop you from even trying, even **breathing properly**. Your head might say, 'I know I should be doing this ...' However, fear stops your body from even attempting it.

Once you understand that, you realise that you don't overcome fear with love. You overcome fear, with ACTION.

Taking ACTION dispels FEAR.

Conversely, IN-ACTION, not doing what you know you should, grows FEAR.

I then took a course of action that has sculpted the rest of my life.

I said to myself, 'Tim, do you know anyone who has done this before?

How did they get through it?!'

Fact was that I didn't know anyone...
Australia seemed so far away. The night somehow got darker, and I began to feel very alone.

Until I began to think 'outside' my own timeline.

I realised then that I did know some men who had done exactly this.

I knew that on a night as dark as this, the original ANZACs came face-to-face with a foe that was waiting for them on their home ground.

What did the ANZACs do? They kept moving forward without letting their fear control them. They kept moving forward without letting their fear control them! Despite hardships, despite a bad situation, despite an enemy intent on killing them.

The outside world could not stop them, from seeing the power inside them.

On ANZAC day we often say, 'Lest we forget ...' But it was like those ANZAC diggers were poking me in the chest saying, 'Lest YOU forget! Lest you forget the power inside you! Lest you forget the power of looking after your mates!'

Even though the beach landing was almost 100 yrs ago, and their stories are told through history books; The ANZACs were right there with me in that moment, and I was no longer alone!

It was like the sun coming up at midnight.

My whole body felt illuminated!

The ANZAC's 1915 'actions', dispelled my 'fear' in 2009.

My actions, then became fearless. I could act and think without fear.

What happened next was one of the **coolest experiences** I have ever had. I literally saw my circulatory system jump out in front of me like a roadmap. I watched my heart pumping blood around my limbs and up to my brain. I thought, 'Really, it's only my brain that needs to keep functioning. If I lose a limb, that's fine, I'll just 'hose clamp it' with a Tourniquet. I can lose a litre of blood no biggie; My brain function will still be solid. It's not like I have to worry about an infection killing me out here.'

So I put **two** tourniquets on my chest in case I lost **more** than one limb.

Now that my body was sorted; Energy started flowing back into my mind. It was like the 'Fear tourniquet' had come off my intelligence.

With fear turned OFF, my intelligence was turned back ON. It told me: 'Tim, on this rough road we are travelling at 20-35kms per hour. RPGs usually self-detonate at 1500m. SO! The ambush will probably start shooting rockets at us from between 800m-1.2km away; this means (if we don't stop) we'll be in the 'kill box' for between 2-4 minutes.'

Now that I was connected 'Internally', I started connecting 'Externally'; To my teammates who were in the vehicle. 'Even if I bleed out and die, 'I said to myself, 'my body is very fit and healthy. I'll have 5 minutes before everything shuts down permanently. By **that** time my **teammates** will revive me with a blood substitute. Obviously, I need to be ready to do the same for them also.'

There was **a lot** of trust in that vehicle.

We've all probably done the 'trust exercise' where you fall backwards and someone catches you? Now, imagine you're standing at the top of a big cliff with jagged rocks at the bottom. Could you fall backwards, trusting only the arms of your colleges to catch you? In this scenario, I trusted that I could **fall into death** and my brothers would **hold me back** from the gates of oblivion. This is where the years of training pays off.

I got my medical kit ready.

With connection restored to my body, mind *and my team*; I had an abundance of energy! Enough to give me **perspective** 'above' my current circumstances.

When we were just about to enter the 'Kill Box' (and to what I thought was my certain death); This empowered attitude told me, 'They might find my body in 5 minutes time, but you know what they're *not* going to find? Magazines full of bullets! I am expending all ammunition on this one ...'

'Actually,' I said to myself,' that's not a bad way to live. Whether I die in five minutes or fifty years' time; I am expending all ammunition. My magazines are full of **bullets**, but my mind is full of **ideas, hopes and dreams**.'

'If I survive this and die in 50 years' time, my body's gonna be just as **dead**. And it won't show that I 'expended all the bullets' of my hopes & dreams; However, dying with a smile, I will!'

Time to start living!

Impossible became **possible** with **energy** through **connection**.

High five!

It was at this point that I learnt another valuable lesson.. but before we get to that, let's lighten the mood, take a breath and talk book tactics.

This book is short, but content-rich.

I recommend you read and **re-read** this book. Having a pencil or highlighter to mark the points that stand out to you is very handy. Even better (ebook) write them down in your own words to be owned then read again in your own time.

A small suggestion; Movement creates **energy**. One scenario for the reader would be to read this book while doing some safe, slow exercise; ie Treadmill, stationary bike, or listening to the audio book when out walking in the fresh air.

Observing certain Universal Truths, I didn't **just** survive dangerous situations, I lived well by them **afterwards**. It's not something I can say I own or created. It existed well **before** I discovered it. This was simple observation, in a simple life story. However, this book isn't an autobiography. I don't like the term 'Self-Help' but that's exactly how I got through tough situations.

I consider myself a regular guy, who discovered some incredible things. These 'things' were always there; I was just lucky enough to 'trip over them'.

I feel 'discovering the obvious' is my story. As a nine year old kid (see below pic), I didn't know I was **dyslexic**. I only ever saw what was **blatantly** obvious. To me it was blatantly obvious that I wasn't smart like everyone else. So I thought, 'If I can't be **smart**, I may as well be **funny**!' Like the label '**Dyslexia**.' Why the heck would you give a hard to spell 'label' to people that **couldn't** spell?!

Tim Thomas at 9 years old. The face of mischief.

This attitude led to **a lot** of classroom antics. When we were taught that our country (Australia) was **'discovered'** by Captain Cook in 1770, I thought 'Australia DISCOVERED!?!? Like something **that big** never existed before they stuck a flag in it?!' To the amusement of my classmates, I asked the teacher, 'Australia is such a big block of dirt. How hard was it discovering **that**?!? Surely, if a boat sailed south long enough they'd hit us!? I dunno, maybe Captain Cook just lost his anchor!?' My classmates cracked up, but the teacher put me in the corner.

In all seriousness, I'm not sharing my story to give a sense that I'm gifted, quite the opposite. I share because sometimes it's easier to learn from **mistakes** when 'other people' are making them.

If you're connecting quickly to what's being said, there's a **good** reason.

The fact is your head already has most of this information. The only **new thing** is how this information is linked together and the pattern revealed. A bit like a 'Dot to Dot' puzzle before the dots are joined. Once the dots are joined everyone then says, 'Oh Look! **Now** I see the pattern!' The pattern was always there, it just needed to be pointed out.

So it is with universal truths; all they need is to be pointed out.

Remember, 'Energy' comes from 'connection.' Once the dots of information in your head are **connected**; empowering (feel-good) energy is created. Once your eyes are opened to these things, there's no closing them again.

However, I encourage you to read this book fully, so you can master and own it **first**, before sharing it with others. In fact, if you do this right, you won't have to search out others to tell. Here's another truth:

Your life is bigger than a billboard.

Other people notice what's going on in your life, (even the stuff you don't want them to see), true story. If you start creating real connections in your own life; energy, power and influence will increase.

This will be noticed. Other people (and opportunities) will often naturally gravitate and want to 'Connect' with you.

I'll talk about how others will react to your self-empowerment a little later. As it's something you will need to be aware of. Getting back to the **most** valuable lesson learned; it's simple but powerful and Chapter Two covers it.

Here we go!

(By the way, you're probably wanting to know what exactly happened the night of the AMBUSH. You can find out the details in an interview I did with ABC's Steve Austin at https://youtu.be/mPuBoj6n7Mc.

2

ENERGY IS LIKE MONEY

How you INVEST IT, determines how much you GET BACK.

Invest your energy well, and you'll live with an abundance

of

it.

Self-mastery gives you more options, happiness and hope,

both now and in the future. As well as an attitude of gratitude.

That's the goal of this book.

However, if you invest your energy poorly, and you'll most

likely live poorly.

Low energy = No options, no hope and no resistance to

other

people's idea of who you are and what you should be doing.

My experience in Afghanistan gave me a small insight into a

bigger picture.

A picture I developed in the subsequent years.

I have spoken to schools, professional sporting teams, business groups, entrepreneurs, community centres and to recovering defence force members about this.

The results have been **incredible**.

However, there is some good news and some great news!

The good news is some changes need to be made.

Why?

Expecting your life to improve by doing **nothing** different is true Sheeple behaviour.

Commercialism tells us, 'Don't change yourself. Just change your TV, Car, clothes or hair.'

PLEASE!

Spending money **won't change** you.

Only YOU change you.

The **great news** is the only 'Start-up capital' you will need is **a heartbeat** and **a name**.

Firstly, 'Heartbeat.'

Being **alive** is a good thing.

After I left the defence force, I opened my own business running outdoor group fitness - boot camps etc. I'd encourage my clients to go **beyond** the workout. If there was anything they wanted to achieve in **any** area of life, they could bring it **closer** by 'working out' with the right attitude.

This created a lot of focus, energy and awareness; However, sometimes more problems.

Some clients would say, 'No matter what I do, I can't make any progress. I'm not achieving my goals and I'm still having **bad days**!'

Interestingly, the boot camps were run on an oval next to a **cemetery**.

I'd direct my client's attention over to the cemetery and ask, 'I wonder what those guys in the ground would give for just **one more day**? Even if it was a bad one? Even if on that day they didn't succeed, and they hurt themselves trying...? What do you think they would give to simply feel **anything**...?'

After some moments of silence I'd add, 'Regardless of how inadequate **we feel**, we are **still** *feeling*. Despite having insecurities, our heart is still beating … We are alive! With living comes **options** and with options, comes **hope**. As your heart beats, your hope continues. This is **your** chance to live. This is the only time that history will allow you, to stamp **your name**, on **your life**.'

Which leads me to the next question;

Why is YOUR NAME so important?

Please put in your FULL NAME in the three blank spaces;

Who is _____ ?

Where is _____ in _____ 's life?

Please give yourself time to ponder these two questions; They're tough questions to ask oneself, but not as tough as a

life lived **in regret**.

This book will start you on an incredible (but somehow very familiar) journey.

It works on the principle that being Adequate is **not** an

option.

Ask yourself **honestly**,

'Am I living my life connected to what I feel is truly **truly important to ME?'**

To Thine own self-be true ... it's often said, but why is it so important?

Is your destiny and happiness a gamble?

Is it dependent on what others say or think of you?

You spend more time with yourself than anyone else.

How much does **your own opinion** count in **your own life**?

Below is what's called a Life Wheel (Fig 1). It's a great tool to see where your life is **currently**, but also **where you'd like it to be.**

To fill it out simply rate yourself (out of ten) in all the different areas of your life. Put an 'X' for where you are **right now** and a 'Tick symbol' for where you'd **ideally like to be.**

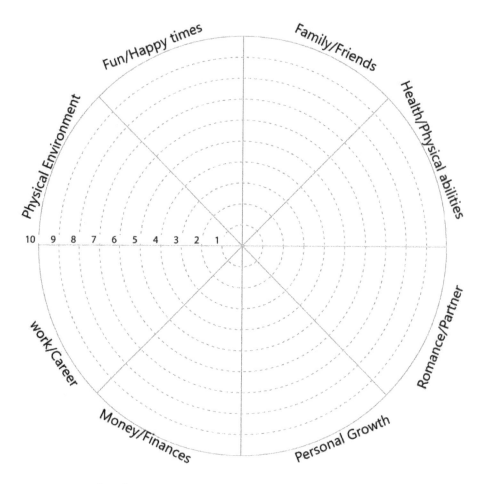

Fig 1. Life Wheel

Once completed, join the X's together and you should see a rough looking circle.

If that circle was a wheel on your car, where would you be continually feeling the bumps?

Hypothetical Question.

Imagine all the sections of your life, to the level you wanted them to be?

Take a moment to imagine what your life would look like? Seriously. You have to see this before anyone can.

What would you see going on that would tell you that you have achieved what you wanted?

What would being in that space 'Feel' like?

Could you get to 'that space if nothing currently changed?

Of course not, **new actions** give us **new outcomes**.

The key to making **permanent** improvements/changes in life, is seeing the **self-benefit** in change.

Seeing 'self-benefit' is a **'game changer.'** It takes you beyond the short-term plan 'mentality'.

The short-term game inevitably leads to **long-term failure**. However, short-term plans are very popular and people pay big bucks for them.

Like the idea of a '12 week health challenge'. Somewhere inside we tell ourselves, 'I can put up with this crap for 12 weeks because I can see an end to it. Then I can get back to whatever I was doing beforehand feeling like I've achieved something.'

How long do you plan on living? 12 weeks or 70-100yrs?

What are 12 weeks going to do, if nothing changes?

Hellooo repeat sales!

Short-term plans are profitable, everywhere and come in a variety of different forms.

They look for people who say; 'I'll escape my problems on a big holiday.' 'I know I'm not a healthy weight, but I'll get in shape for my wedding or high school reunion.' 'I know my marriage is in trouble but I'll do an intensive weekend couple's

therapy to make up for it.' Whilst none of these activities

are

without benefit, you'd be mistaken if you thought that something **outside you** could do all the work **for you**.

Spending money won't change you, only **YOU** will change **you**.

3

CHANGE

In the above picture you'll see me in Afghanistan, this time with coffee cooking gear around me.

I'd bring coffee to the guys and make sure they had a smile on their faces before I left.

This didn't happen naturally. It happened because of a changed **head and heart** space.

A change that permanently affected all my actions from that point on.

Unknowingly, I was working towards something … **my destiny**.

So, what does coffee have to do with 'Self Benefit' and 'Change'?

The life wheel (in the previous chapter) works in **real time** and what follows is an excellent example of it.

Two weeks prior to that photo, I was in a **very different** head and heart space.

Our Commando company had been 'outside the wire' in Afghanistan for several weeks.

This meant often going days and weeks with just an hour or two of sleep.

Currently I'm sitting comfortably at my laptop and it's easy to write about my war service. However, I remember back to

those moments … Every part of you **hurts!** Not just the physical parts. You're away from home and family. On deployment, you're solely hanging out with grown men in a combat environment for months. The energy that comes from being with a beautiful woman and smiling kids simply isn't there.

It's kinda like your soul dries out a little bit every day.

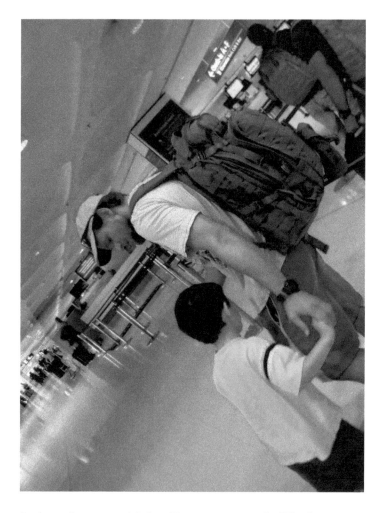

It doesn't pay to think of home too much. The last memory of your young child was at the airport. They were holding onto your pants crying, **gasping for breath**, trying to stop you leaving. When you walked away to board the flight. Their last words were in anguish. My five year old son screamed **a lung full of air** in every word, '**DADDY … DON'T … GO!!**'

Considering that I genuinely thought I wasn't going to return, it was a bloody hard day for both of us.

As a soldier, we get trained to **ignore pain**, and yes this was the job I willingly signed up for. However, that doesn't mean I'm heartless or I feel nothing …

Day and night a Commando's work is high tempo, arduous and very dangerous.

We were shot at, rocketed, mortared and ambushed **daily**.

I remember the day after we lost a man to an IED (Improvised Explosive Device). My team was so fatigued that
we started arguing with each other.

Friction is **very** draining in a small team, especially when you're **together 24/7**.

On that point, getting angry at someone when you're

already
fatigued, is like spending $1000 when you only have $10 in the
bank. It puts you further into debt …

In previous civilian jobs, I could knock off and go home. Didn't matter what my problems were. It didn't matter how tough the day was, my job didn't own me. It didn't stop me hanging out with friends, or doing leisure activities.

In fact, that was how I started dealing (or not dealing) with

all

my problems.

Unknowingly, I'd compensate for any problem I had by having more **fun** or **consuming** or **buying** something extra.

Unfortunately, distractions **aren't** solutions.

All this did was stop me from learning what I needed to;

and

what's more, it stopped me reaching my full potential.

I didn't know, and couldn't see how my very **own actions** were sabotaging my potential.

Some call this **invisible karma**.

Karma is an awareness of 'you get what you give'.

Invisible Karma is **unawareness** of how your actions are affecting others (and yourself). You're completely **blind** to how **your actions** are affecting others and the damage it's

42

doing to yourself.

Invisible Karma is often obvious to everyone **except that individual.**

For me, it was easy to surround myself with enabling friends who would agree with my view of the world.

Scarily, I could have spent my whole life like that.

Comfort zones are great, but **nothing grows there**.

My full potential would never be reached, and (painfully) I'd never know why! I'd just have this sense that something **wasn't quite right**; maybe I'd drink more to compensate.

Fortunately, (painfully) Afghanistan didn't allow me distractions.

Outside the wire, in a war zone, there's no coffee shop or

pubs
around to decompress your head. No home or family nearby, and no enabling friends.

It was this isolation that brought me (**forced me**) to reshape my thinking about life.

It actually gave me an instinctive use of what I later discovered as the aforementioned **life wheel**.

So one day, after an argument with my boss about nothing, my vehicle commander told me to 'P*ss off' to do some time in the gun turret.

Previous to the RPG ambush, I was keeping watch. I remember thinking, 'What's the point? I was running on empty two weeks ago and now everything I do is being criticised. Why make the effort? There is no point. My team is turning on itself and I have a feeling I'm going to **die soon**.' This was previous to being cut off in the RPG ambush.

If I was to fill out the 'Life Wheel' right there, it'd be ZEROES all around.

I didn't even have the desire for a better outcome!

Easier to lay down and die…

Part of me was **dying**.

However, part of me **had to die**.

Escaping from my problems no longer worked.

Buying more 'stuff' made me feel better, but it didn't solve anything.

That moment in the gun turret, it was like I had only two cents worth of energy …

What happened next changed my world.

I thought,

'If two cents of energy is all I have,

I had better invest that wisely!'

But what options were available?

In the life wheel, there are what's called **universal levers**.

These universal levers are sections in the wheel of life, that if improved, they will (in time) benefit **everything** else.
One of the universal levers is your **physicality**, your health, your body.

Which is very handy as it is the **one thing we can control**.
Unfortunately, my body was soo fatigued I couldn't work any harder. Plus my pain in the arse boss was making life very difficult.
Since I couldn't improve the quality of my performance, I instead invested in improving the **quality of my rest**.

'Outside the wire' in Afghanistan, we never got anything that you could call quality rest or sleep. It was a war zone. Most guys would crash exhausted on the ground whenever it was allowed or safe to do so.

So this is how the Universal lever of **'quality rest'** changed everything for me.

Yes, I was exhausted, but before I laid flat to sleep; I would take a few minutes (that small two cents worth of energy) to do some slow, deep breathing & stretching. I'd never done breathwork before, but instinctively these were the motions I was going through before resting. It was this moment, as a hurting & fatigued soldier (breathing deeply in bed) that 14 years later would create BREATHWORK IN BED. *See end of chapter for the very basic but effective Breathwork in Bed techniques I used in Afghanistan. Alternatively, use: www.breathworkinbed.com.au search the app store for 'Breathwork in Bed'. (Launch date is Dec 2023)

Looking back, this was the **tipping point** for me. Everything that happened after this, happened as a result of **breathwork improving my rest**; Investing that two cents worth of energy into my Breathwork, gave me better rest and more energy. I woke to feel less fatigued,, and to someone who's feeling like they have nothing, that's really something! I turned two cents into six cents worth of energy!

I kept investing and reinvesting my newly found **'energy capital'** into better quality rest, until the day I woke and realised that I now could start investing in my performance.

So each day I'd do some extra push ups and sit ups.

This gave me more energy **capital** for my busy day.

I was becoming energised and **in control** underneath my own skin.

> Once **inside myself** was better; I was in a much better position to improve things **outside myself**.

I still had a team that argued and a boss that made life hard. I could be having a good day, but if **my team** was having a bad day,

> I'd be dragged into it.

However, that little bit of extra energy gave me **perspective**. I started seeing all actions in terms of **energy cost**.

Long story short; I discovered that most energy wastage actually came from, myself.

Yes, I hated my boss, he was fussy about things that I didn't think were relevant. However, there was a lesson I had been refusing to learn, and it was **costing me dearly** (invisible Karma).

The lesson I had been refusing to learn was this;

The world is the way it is, and **not** the way I want it to be...

People are the way they are, and **not** the way I want them to be...

They're not bad people, they're just **other** people, and **other** people have **other** priorities.

Jeez, Tim did you have to go all the way to Afghanistan to learn that!?

YES. Actually.

Surprisingly, I discovered that it cost far less energy doing what my boss wanted **willingly** without an argument.

It didn't stop there.

With my boss happy, all the energy I wasted arguing with him was now **available,** and ready to be invested **elsewhere.**

My team needed help.

Like I said before, I could be having a good day, but if my team wasn't, then I wasn't either.

My team's safety was always a priority. However, I had to make their **welfare** (their head space) a priority also.

I then focussed my extra energy into making my team's life better. **Helping others** affected me also. Suddenly, my own problems didn't seem so big.

Funny that.

Using universal levers created more personal energy for myself.

That energy started **overflowing** into other areas of my life.

Things were looking up.

As my energy and influence grew, so did my awareness.

I noticed that there was still a lot of friction **in other teams**. We were a Company strength Commando unit, (so you're looking at 50-60 operators with attached support units)

What could I do for so many people? I was a just Private. Lowest in the food chain. Paid to do what everyone **else** wanted.

However, I read a quote from someone long since dead and it got me thinking:

'I am only one person, but I am still **a person**. I can't do much, but what I can do, **I should do** and by the grace of God, **I will do**.' (Edward Hale 1822-1909)

Back then **Breathwork in Bed** wasn't an app, I couldn't give it to people; It wasn't even on my radar. Breathwork for me was done out of survival. I wasn't in a position to teach anybody this. However, I do have a supply of fresh coffee.' I thought to myself, 'I could give that to the guys…?'

But that's when I hit my next big obstacle.

You think making coffee for someone else sounds easy right!?

Allow me to explain the situation I was in, and the '*unique*' personality dynamic of Special Forces.

In any group dynamic, you have several different personality types. Male & female, talkers & listeners, dominant & submissive, etc. They mostly balance each other out.

However, Special Forces are, euphemistically 'Special …'

Imagine a group of one million men.

Then from that group filter out the top 500 Alpha male personalities.

Then select out from that 500, the individuals with the highest level of physical and mental ability (with a 'Never Say Die' attitude thrown in).

You'd probably end up with 50.

Imagine 50 highly capable, competitive and dominant Alpha males in **one group?**

That's about the size of a Commando Company.

We can achieve **incredible things** - when we're not metaphorically killing each other!

Getting back to seeing the self-benefit in making coffee …

In that 'Special dynamic' I knew that any act of undeserved 'kindness/service' to a dominant ALPHA, could result in me being considered **'below them'**, less than equal, a servant.

I was no-one's servant!

I'd gotten to where I had in the Commando Unit because I'd always taken the path less travelled. The road of physically tougher and harder choices.

Before I joined the Commandos I was a NO RULES fighter for six years in the 1990s. This was before it was even called

MMA. I'd always chose to fight opponents who were stronger and more skilled than me.

Here's me about to get hit in the face in the 90s. Back then they called it NO RULES fighting. Notice we didn't even have gloves!?

Why did I fight guys who'd probably beat me?

For me it **wasn't** about winning; It was about getting **stronger**.

I had **no idea** of what my full potential was. I just knew I'd never reach it by fighting people of equal or **lesser ability**.

The more outside my physical comfort zone I put myself, the stronger and more energised I became.

The benefits of this were more than physical. However, I did notice that I **wouldn't** get out of my physical comfort zone **willingly**.

I needed an environment that gave me **no other choice**. Namely, if I knew that I'd be soon fighting a stronger and more skilled opponent; I'd have a lot more motivation to train extra hard.

This developed one section of my life wheel, but it also benefited others.

Unfortunately, I became overly specialised.

Playing to our strengths and not our weaknesses is an easy thing to fall into.

As guys, we love getting compliments on the physical work we can DO. That is, problem solve, fix things, make things, excel at sports, etc. If someone tells us we need to improve ourselves, we just redirect their focus to all the awesome stuff we CAN DO. The stuff that other people value us for doing.

I thought that being extra good in one area of my life would balance out all of the others.

Hello Invisible Karma.

Unfortunately, being good physically didn't excuse me from being underdeveloped **emotionally**.

Bringing Coffee to the guys, and being seen as a servant, was pushing me outside my emotional comfort zone.

I knew that when I'd bring Coffee to my fellow Alpha Commandos I'd get called '**The Brew Bitch**'.

No way, **not** gonna happen.

Did someone say the big obstacles are **inside** you?

Would getting out of my 'emotional comfort zone' be as beneficial as getting out of my physical one?

Remember:

Change only happens when we see the self-benefit …

I might have been becoming **energised**, but I saw no benefit in being seen as **less** than equal.

'Stuff that, I've worked too hard to get to where I am!' I'd tell myself. 'If I go to the effort of making coffee for a group of guys, and they call me 'Brew Bitch' ... Call the medic, someone's getting politely **knocked out!**'

However, guys were still fatigued and arguing.

If the situation was to change, I had to. I had to find the self-benefit in this simple act of bringing them coffee.

I tried focussing on the needs of the guys, but that wasn't enough.

I then asked myself, 'Who did I want around me when good times turn bad? Do I want fatigued, disconnected men? Or do I want a strong, connected group of guys that are ready to fight together as a cohesive force?'

That's when it came to me.

'Their Strength is **my** strength.'

It doesn't matter if they like, hate or talk badly about me. If I do an 'act of service', they're **stronger**; and that means **I'm stronger**!

So here's what happened as a result;

I brought freshly made coffee to the other teams.
Yep - I got called the 'Brew Bitch'. I wasn't a fan of it.

However, there is an advantage of living in close quarters all the time. You can **observe** the result of your actions when you're **not** there. I'd go back to my own team area and watch the guys drinking the fresh coffee that I'd just brought them. After the first sip, they'd realise that this was really **fresh coffee**, and then they'd just, **stop** …

Everything would just **stop** …

The arguing, the tension, the anxiety, all stopped …

I'd see broad shoulders relaxing as if a great weight had been lifted. Their gaze would look up and drift off to a far horizon; Then they'd take in a **deep slow breath,,** & that was **worth noting**! They were instinctively **self regulating with breath**!

For a few moments, they were not in a war zone. They were back home in a coffee shop relaxing with friends.

And that's when I heard it …

The Whisper.

(It gets **freaky** here and I won't blame you for thinking I've gone crazy)

But I definitely heard an audible whisper!

It could have been a result of my fatigue, stress or lack of sleep, but it came from behind me (slightly to my right).

It was gentle, calm and I had the sense it was well-intentioned.

It whispered,

'Take the ego out of it.'

It made the hairs on my neck stand up. It seemed like insanity, but what happened, as a result, was undeniable.

I realised that investing my **own** energy in **me**, only got me so far.

This whisper was there to take me to the next level.

Time to stop wasting energy on **ego**.

Strangely, all the actions I did from that point on were very familiar to me; however, this time I was doing everything with a **servant's heart**.

This **freed me** in ways unimaginable.

Imagine living life and having 0% energy wasted on what others thought or said about you? Or who was looking at you?

This is freedom!

Besides, what the hell was I over there fighting for!? If not for freedom.

I termed it the 'Ego bridge'. If you drop your **Ego**, it becomes a **bridge to anything** you want to achieve.

Here's what happened next.

I kept investing in my own quality rest and exercise. However, this time it was done without **ego**.

I accumulated an abundance of strength, but this time it wasn't for status; it was for service.

Strength is for service, not status.

(Jeez, Tim! Did you have to go to Afghanistan to learn that??)

Yes actually.

I was becoming 'Wisely Selfish'.

Soon, it wasn't just my team mates who wanted coffee. The Officers wanted it also.

This made it another level of difficult. You see, that's like your boss coming into the workers lunch room and taking the snacks.

The coffee was the one pleasure we 'workers' owned.

However, the Whisper did say, 'Take the ego out of it' and who am I not to listen to the whisper of the universe (or insanity). So, that's exactly what I did!

I made coffee for the officers, and then something amazing happened.

Everyone sat down and **talked together**.

Bosses and workers talked, like real human beings.

Open discussion and laughter among all ranks.

Problems were solved, resources were allocated, **sh*t got done!**

There weren't any orders given, no snide remarks, no lingering malice and **no ego**!

Holy Smacking Duck Sh*T! (Tim's mind just got blown)

Was this what the whisper was for?

In those few moments of **ego free** conversation, we got more done than months of orders and arguing.

It was like one of those biblical moments with the angels singing, 'AAaahhh AAAA..'

I was the lowest rank in the room and yet became the most influential man there.

Right then I saw the **power** of servanthood; not servitude, but *servanthood.*

Sure, it didn't stop the fact that the enemy was still out there and there were dark times ahead. However, we knew that when the dark times came, we would look at each other and be strengthened. When the enemy does attack, they will find 50 of the fiercest fighting men on the planet, **fighting as one!**

I felt like yelling out, 'THIS, IS, SPARTA!' But then everyone would laugh at the private making coffee.

'Breathwork in Bed's origin story isn't fancy. It started with just me (fatigued as hell) laying in the desert dirt of Afghanistan; Following what felt instinctive on a thin foam mat. As much as my body was screaming for sleep, I'd take the time to stretch out. Just the muscles that were really hurting (usually hamstrings, shoulders, neck and lower back) for 20-30secs per muscle, while taking deep slow breaths; IE Holding the stretch while inhaling through the nose for 5 secs, then exhale (through nose and mouth) for 5 secs. After breathing & stretching away my physical pain, I'd then lay on my back; When firing a weapon, I'd always take a deep breath, exhale & hold, focusing on my right trigger finger. On this occasion, I'd focus 100% on my left thumb nail & take a deep nasal breath into it for 5 secs. I'd picture breathing 'light and tension' into it, and then exhaling out the tension & light from that left thumb nail. I'd then move onto my left pointer finger & repeat the process with every finger nail. If I wasn't asleep after that, I'd start the same process on my toes. This was a very basic, but an effective technique that 14 years later, would lead me to create Breathwork in Bed. *For more breathwork techniques pls visit www.breathworkinbed.com.au *side note* Writing this, I am just now overcome with a strange feeling. Looking back on that young man in 2009, in the dark, far from home, breathing in his bed; I can see that he was a truly determined little F*kker. That kid would forfeit his life to serve his country; Right now, in 2023, it's a weird sensation for me to have this perspective; However, I am kinda glad I survived. If you believe in alternate realities, I am sure there is a reality where I didn't survive. I often wondered why I did survive, when men **far better** than me did not. However, in this reality I did survive and I am writing to you right now. Figure that one out!?

4
HOOK ME UP!

Could we do with **more** good energy? Yes?

After all, it's good to feel good.

Before this happens, we need to have a better understanding of ourselves.

As human's we're more like **solar panels** than **generators**.

In the way that we receive our **energy**, from what we connect to.

For example, when you exercise (for the right reason), you connect with your own body and become energised.

Remember what I said about the goal of fear isn't to scare you, it's to immobilise you?

This makes the opposite of fear, 'action and movement'.

Movement and Action dispel fear.

Conversely, inactivity **breeds fear**.

Inactivity is the perfect breeding ground for those small gnawing fears to grow into something that could eventually control **you** and **your destiny**.

This is how it's possible, for two different attitudes, to live in the same body on different days.

One that is connected and energised, and one that is disconnected and flat.

Same life, but with

two completely different destinies.

Unfortunately, there is no middle ground. It's either a life that's going up or a life that is going down.

Once you become connected 'inside yourself', you have a better chance of connecting to what is 'outside yourself'.

Imagine two people looking up at the stars.

Person A is fatigued. They see nothing more than a bunch of random shiny lights.

Person B is energised. Energised enough to be aware of things outside themselves. They see that the stars have patterns (or they listened when it was pointed out). This pattern is then used to navigate themselves. They can effectively get themselves **anywhere** they want to go and not get lost.

Person A's fatigue, risks them walking aimlessly around in circles.

Life can be view from a very similar stand point.

Fatigued people see life as only a bunch of random events, 'Stuff just happens to me.'

However, if you can **see** the patterns in everyday events, (or **listen** when it's pointed out) you can work in harmony with that knowledge. Not walking in circles, but successfully navigating your way anywhere you want to go. In this case, if you ever get lost or lose your way, take the time to slow down and look inwards (connecting to your inner **truth**). Then look **outwards**, to align yourself with what's important, so you can *'walk the inner talk'.*

When you 'walk the inner talk', even when you do struggle and fall, you're going to be falling in the **right** direction. Even your failures push you in the right direction! What a comforting thought!

I didn't make the stars or patterns in life, and I don't claim to understand them fully. I don't have to! You don't need a great intellect to join the dots on a 'Dot to Dot' puzzle.

> You don't have to be **smart or gifted** to have an **empowered life.**

Once you see the patterns for yourself, it's easy to navigate by them and then (joyfully) point them out to others.

Problem is, (like I said earlier) if you let yourself become fatigued; You won't see the pattern, and you'll find yourself **walking around in circles**.

Doing the same stuff repeatedly and unfortunately, working harder won't get you what you want.

This is the whole reason I created **Breathwork in Bed**. To allow people access to a simple app on their phones which is aimed at **getting out** of the 'thoughtless fatigue cycle'. There's a lot of people (Sheeple) doing it, so it does seems normal. Working harder, but somehow everything you want, is getting further away.

Without direction, we tell ourselves, 'If I just work harder into this circle, I'll get what I want.' Then we make the BIG mistake of connecting our 'sense of self-worth' to our circle.

Then a bigger mistake of comparing it to others.

'My circle is soo much better than yours.' Alternately 'That person's circle has more money in it. I don't want my circle to feel less important. Therefore, I need to **change** my circle to be **more like theirs**.'

Succeed or fail you're still walking in circles …

and it's **exhausting**!

It is possible to live a whole life like this. You will survive, but an imbalance is created, and passed on.

The feeling of 'Something's not quite right' is ever present.

Our consumer society loves it when we are exhausted and unbalanced.

It knows this is the first step in making People into Sheeple;

True story!

The marketers get us when we're low, by saying, 'I know you're tired and looking for answers. You deserve a break from your problems. So here's what I'll do for you. I'll solve all your problems (albeit temporarily) in exchange for your hard earned cash. If your problems get bigger, simply make more money to buy more solutions.'

PLEASE!!!

Once you see this lie, (and it's everywhere) it's easy to see, and then see through it.

Being '**Self**-empowered' means you don't need '**External**-empowerment.'

Why pay someone else to do a job you can do yourself?!

This is why real deal 'self-empowerment' is so incredibly rare.

This world makes a lot of money from promising, **but not** delivering – that is, creating repeat business: 'Why make one sale, when you can make 1000s?'

If someone was to truly 'Self Empower' me; then that's exactly what I'd be able to do; self-empower **myself**. I wouldn't have to keep going back for more. In fact, the person who empowered me initially, is now no longer **needed**. I may still check in from time to time, but I don't need repeat sales. Why?

Real self-empowerment, doesn't have a middleman.

Consciously or not, we are all trying to balance out our energy shortages. Every wondered why you drank more after a bad day of work? Had to buy that 'pretty item' when you're feeling sad? If we don't see this in ourselves, our consumer society **certainly will and take full advantage of it**! Visualise this for yourself;

Imagine the 'YOU' with poor diet, no exercise, no breathwork in bed, a resultant bad night's sleep and arguing with people close to you …

Sure you could put up with it for a period of time, but eventually, you'd become unbalanced. This would lead to being drained, exhausted, cranky, hurting those closest to you, and worst-case scenario, pushing them away from you (sometimes forever!)

Conversely, imagine the 'YOU' when eating clean, exercising, doing **breathwork in bed**, having a great night's sleep and feeling warmly connected to those close to you.

Which person would have a higher chance of needing a short- term energy fix? Which person would be more easily influenced by marketers promising false hope?

Plus, honestly, which person has a higher chance of being an asshole? Keep in mind that sending out negative energy, attracts negative energy to you. People in this drained energy state often feel like the world has turned against them.

If we don't understand or manage our own energy, fatigue turns us from People into **Sheeple**.

Once you see it, you'll start seeing it everywhere.

In the short term, it's far more profitable for the marketers to keep people as Sheeple.

Interesting fact: We have 7.4 billion fellow human beings on this planet.

Globally $435 billioni is spent on illegal drugs.

Remember, in exchange for your cash, this world will happily provide you with easy, temporal fixes. Short-term energy loans that help you get by today, make you feel balanced, but tomorrow you must pay it all back and with **interest**. Hence the guaranteed repeat business.

Did someone say, 'Walking in circles'?

Drug and alcohol abuse are obvious and extreme examples of profiteering from the human desire to find balance. However, have you ever wondered WHY we get so fatigued and imbalanced?

This question is the key to unlocking **rare** knowledge.

Ever seen a donkey motivated by a carrot dangled on a string in front him? The donkey's desire for that carrot keeps him moving in a direction that he probably **wouldn't** otherwise choose to go in. The more the donkey runs, the hungrier he gets. The hungrier he gets, the more he runs; and he soon becomes exhausted, but all he can think about is the stupid carrot!

We shouldn't laugh.

We humans have our own 'carrots' we chase; and we get very confused as to **why** we can't catch these 'dangled carrots'.

Unfortunately, this is where our natural human desires get used **against** us by very clever marketing to move us in directions we wouldn't otherwise go in.

Dangled Carrots are everywhere.

'You want the **Happiness carrot**, don't you? You can have it! However, first, you need to chase the carrots of money, power, car, house, pool, career. If you're not happy it's because you don't have enough of the former.'

'Do you want the Carrot of feeling **loved** and highly valued? First, chase the carrot of **social acceptance**. You know, look like this, own that, be seen with these people, eating this and driving that. If you don't feel loved it's because you're not worth anything without the approval of others.'

Even our most powerful desire, our desire to be with the

right

person, gets dangled as a carrot. The idea that buying or owning something will help you find your soul mate?! This concept is particularly offensive and toxic, but it's out there. I tell my own children, 'Good face and clothes doesn't always make for a good relationship.'

In fact, finding the right person for you, your soul mate, is

the

most specialised niche market you'll ever experience.

Think about this…

There are **billions** of people on this planet,

and there is only **one** you.

Who do you want to be with?

Who are you trying to appeal to?

Billions, or **just one**?   73

If you want to **find** the right person, you have to start **being** the right person.

The true you. The empowered you.

I've observed that the more empowered a person is, the more gravity they have to draw the right people into their circle. Out of this circle, you choose 'The One' right for you.

Just on that, I do believe we need to be particularly gentle with our fellow human beings. They're exactly like us, **but not us**. They have **their own** priorities and needs. However, just like us, they live in the same demanding world and their energy is **just as limited**. Can two solar panels turn to each other for 100% of their energy?

So be gentle on one another.

Getting back to Carrot chasing.

'Do you have a dream? Something you always wanted to achieve? Great, but don't think you can do it without using our carrot products. I mean, how many carrots would you chase for your dream to come true?'

Becoming **exhausted** carrot chasing is inevitable, and our consumer society **loves it** when we are. It's like a loan shark being happy that you're broke.

Selling 'quick fix' energy to exhausted humans is again, **very** profitable. 'Exploitation of Sheeple', (or what I call the **'Expleeple** Industry') sells exhausted people short-term

fixes.

Fatigued Sheeple don't have a chance. Examples of this are everywhere …

Caffeinated Energy drinks. USD $55 billion dollars spent annuallyii.

Coffee. Over 2250,000,000 cups of coffee are consumed

daily around the worldiii.

Personally, I don't have a problem with consuming a timely and appropriate amount of any of the above products.

However, **buy** the product, otherwise the product will **buy you**. You may have been tired before you had it, but now you have it, you must have it daily. Without it, you can't even be a nice person.

It's funny, but all these energy supplements have the hallmarks of an **abusive relationship**. I mean, no one ever deliberately gets into an abusive relationship. Abusive relationship never **start** with abuse. They first get seduced by sweet promises, but then slowly the initial rewards get replaced by **punishments**. The longer the abusive relationship lasts, the greater the punishment is for noncompliance. Before you know it, **fear of punishment** replaces any initial positive experience. Energy supplements behave in exactly the same way. If you don't do what they expect of you (and they expect daily consumption), they punish you with headaches/migraines, stress, anxiety, lethargy, irritability, depression, muscle stiffness, flu-like symptoms, insomnia and brain fog … but somehow this is acceptable because why?

Everyone is doing it…

This is how the population of Sheepleville lives.

If you don't find a way to fulfil your own needs, someone else will, and the cost will be far greater than the money you pay for it.

This has happened throughout the ages …

However, **exhaustion** can be the best thing that ever happens to a person. Why? Exhaustion (if viewed correctly) gives us an opportunity to **break** the cycle.

Exhaustion asks us two simple questions,

'Do I keep going?'

Or, 'Do I change the way I do things?'

Remember **real energy** (like your breath) is already

inside you.

The choices we make increase or decrease it.

Cultivate it right, and it can create ANYTHING.

This is how you know it's real … **Real Energy** is a universal currency that can be used to create anything. It can make happiness, better relationships, better grades, motivation and wealth (yes money). It can give you gratitude for what you have, bring your dreams into reality, open your eyes to things you've never seen before, heal, strengthen families, even get a better night's sleep … and the best thing is **real energy** does all this **naturally**! Just remember, it's generally not instantaneous (like an Energy drink), but far more powerful. A bit like flicking on a light switch is quicker than waiting for the sun to rise. The light switch (energy fix) is instantaneous, but the Sun (your wisely invested energy lifestyle) is far more powerful, beautiful, lasting and free!!

However, everything valuable needs to be **protected**.

Boundaries need to be put in place and guarded. Why? Substances aren't the only thing that people use to find balance.

In energy deficient soil, some plants become carnivorous. It can be similar in humans.

Personality types evolve from energy deficient environments.

Out of balance Sheeple often use/abuse other Sheeple and people to satisfy their own deficiencies.

Instead of developing methods to empower **themselves**, methods are developed to disempower or **take** from others.

Most have had experience with an 'Energy thief'. A person who **takes** energy from us. A skilled 'energy thief' can put in us, the **fear** of it happening again ...

'Being Taken from' can leave you feeling like you've been damaged beyond repair.

Remember, the goal of fear isn't to scare you, it's to immobilise you.

Energy Thieves can immobilise a person **permanently**.

Some Energy Thieves are completely unaware they're doing it. However, others are very skilled. Making manipulating others into an art form.

Many people have stopped their 'Self-empowerment' journey because they didn't expect (or know how to react to) Energy Thieves.

The opposite of fear isn't Love, it's **action**.

Taking effective **action** comes from understanding how the **'Dark Side'** of energy works.

The next chapter is about dealing with the Dark Side, and it's **critical** to your survival and growth.

5

DEALING WITH THE DARK SIDE

'Luke, I am your Father!'

'NOOOOooooooooooo!'

Didn't expect **that**, did he?!

There's a lot of positive talk about 'Self-Empowerment.' But no one ever tells you that there's an **unexpected** bad/dark side.

There's a good reason the path less travelled is, **less** travelled.

There's a lot of unexpected difficulties. Things that no one will tell you about.

Luke Skywalker initially thought to become a Jedi was about experimenting with his cool new powers (the Force). Until he encountered the Dark Side; and that's when things **got real.**

It'd be a very **big** mistake to think that 'empowering yourself' isn't without difficulty or opposition.

This chapter is dedicated to getting you **through** a part of the journey where most people **stop** because of the unexpected difficulties.

Something is coming your way …

If you learn about it now, you'll not just 'deal with it' but be able to use it to your advantage.

The problem is that when you start becoming 'Self Empowered' you're breaking a few **societal rules** (invisible rules Sheeple unconsciously follow).

Rules that you probably didn't know existed **until** you broke them.

Unfortunately, you don't know how strong the current is until you start to swim **against it**.

Going against 'the flow' often means going against the **flock**.

Expect resistance from people and places you **least** expected.

This chapter draws heavily on my talks I give to high school students.

When I'm talking with high school students, I spend **a lot of time** explaining what to expect in the **initial** stages of their growth. I do this because the peer pressure at this age is so intense that it can condition a teenager to **a lifetime** of unproductive thought.

First up I need to break any accepted negative behaviours that would impede growth. I do this by dealing with any threats/bullies (Energy Thieves) in the room on the day.

In front of the group, I take a sapling in my hand and I say, 'Look at this small sapling. The seed had enough good soil to stick its head up and start growing.

'This is very symbolic of where most people start. People start to bring their dreams into reality. Sadly, this is the stage where most people stop.

'This beautiful and delicate young tree could grow into anything; it could make healthy fruit or might even provide a cure for cancer. Who knows, right!?'

I then get up close to the group members; Look them straight in the eye and ask the students, 'Do you feel like ripping a leaf off it? No? Are you sure? It's really easy because it hasn't become a big tree yet. It's still small and vulnerable.'

I then ask a group question, 'Who has ever said something nasty and cutting about someone else? In fact, who has said hurtful things to someone in this very room?!'

A lot of hands go up, and stay up …

I then address the plant with a vindictive tone, 'Hey, you look disgusting … You don't belong here … Everyone is saying you are such a loser.' After each insult, I rip a few small leaves off and throw them away.

Then I turn to the group and in a clean voice ask, 'What's going to happen if I keep ripping leaves of this small plant?'

The high school students usually answer, 'It will never grow.'

or

'It's alive, but dying slowly.'

A small silence is given to allow the gravity of what's being said to sink in. I then continue, 'You might not even **like** this kind of tree, but if you don't let it grow you'll never see what it **could be**. It might just make a medical breakthrough 'fruit' that could benefit you and your family, but **you** stopped it from growing by ripping its leaves off at this very early stage...'

'Understand this, if you damage **others**, you're actually damaging **yourself**. If you allow others to **grow**, you will be allowing **yourself to grow** also!'

The following is taken from my high school talks regarding the 'dark side' and 'Energy Thieves'.

*

'This is why **the initial stage** of growth is so hard. We have all been taken from ... and it's easy to continue accepting this behaviour; which is why you must understand Energy Thieves **before** you become one yourself.

Energy Thieves **are real** and everyone here has experienced them on some level. They steal energy from others. They hurt others. Just for a second, think of the person that constantly hurts you, or that you are fearful of hurting you again?

Energy Thieves, instead of using their energy to **grow** themselves, they become really good at **taking** from others.

Energy Thieves are **small**, but they know how to make you **feel smaller**. This is so they can appear bigger and more intimidating in comparison.

In a sealed environment like a school, it's a technique that is very powerful but make no mistake, you **can't grow** on insecurity.

Energy Thieves are like this Venus flytrap, they often come from very poor soil, and as much as they are good at taking, they never grow that big ...

There are two very different types of people in this world and they are both you.'

Holding up the Venus fly trap and the sapling tree to the students, I continue. 'There's the **'You'** that keeps their branches in the sun and can outgrow anything. Then there's the **'You'** that takes from others. Funny thing is they both start the **same size**, but they have **very** different potentials

. . .

So how do you beat Energy Thieves?

From understanding how they work, and this will take effort.

You might think they don't deserve you spending your valuable energy on them. However, think of it as spending $5 now to save $10,000 later.

Personally, I've had my butt kicked and been hurt by others on a number of levels (emotional, physical, mental, financial). When it happened, I thought, 'What do I do now?' Instinctively, I'd like to go after this person and **take back** what was taken from me; Then I thought, 'The only reason this energy thief took from me is because they feel inadequate. They're a Zero. They appear strong right now, but their potential is limited. Limited to the number of victims they can find. Like a parasite that needs to feed off a host.'

If I go after them, I'll give the best of my energy away for absolutely no return and in the process become another zero myself!

However, I can use this negative experience to **focus and increase** my own strengthening process. A negative experience doesn't stop me investing in myself. I'm going to get stronger and stronger. It's now just a matter of time before I **outgrow** that energy thief!

Think of it this way; I'm sure to **a fly**, a Venus flytrap is terrifying. However, the fly will always be a fly. As humans, we need to maximize our unique human abilities. As, unlike the fly, we're not in a **fixed and finite state of awareness**. We can grow, strengthen and develop ourselves. Imagine if the fly could grow and develop itself into a bird; then from a bird into a cat; then from a cat, into a **lion** … Now, imagine that **lion**, walking past the same Venus fly trap …? It would laugh at itself, thinking of how it ever saw that as a real threat!

Start to see **all** your current problems as 'Venus flytraps' **in the making**.

Start seeing all problems as fantastic opportunities to strengthen yourself and out-grow it.

This is how it is for people who can 'Self-Empower' **themselves**.

They still have problems, but they view it from the future **lion's perspective**.

Small minded people will always have **big** problems. Why?

It's the same problem but viewed **very** differently.

Having this knowledge doesn't stop bad things happening or Energy Thieves from taking from you.

However, it greatly **reduces** their effectiveness.

For example, if you only had $1.50 worth of energy and someone took a whole $1. That's a **massive** withdrawal. You can't help but react, want to claw it back and then defend what's left.

However, if your goal was focus on strengthening yourself, to create an abundance within yourself; Instead of just $1.50, you'd have, say $1500. If the same person took a $1, you wouldn't overreact (as you're now connected to something greater than them). You'd just say, 'That's all you're getting. You've just shown your true colours and you've just missed out on the rest of my life. You can stay here and play with

that

dollar, I'm not going to waste $5 to try and get it back; I'm simply moving forward.'

Moving forward/empowering yourself becomes the **only** choice when you **realise** that whether you empower yourself or not; Energy Thieves will always, **always** try and take from you. It's what they do. It's **all they can do**. Some take so naturally, they themselves can't see that they are taking from others. So don't waste energy trying to point it out to them.

Just remember, they don't, and never will, **own** what's

under

your skin, in your head or what's in your heart. They **can't stop** you outgrowing them … and you don't need their permission.

You'll only need to outgrow them once. True story!

So why is the initial phase of growth soo hard?

Shouldn't everyone be happy I'm growing and developing myself?

What are we not understanding here?

Why is there so much resistance to us becoming 'Self-empowered' people? Surely that's a good thing?!

Two reasons why Energy Thieves are against your growth;

Firstly, while you are still small, you're an easy meal. Easy to take from and intimidate (as we saw in the first example of ripping leaves off the sapling). Energy Thieves see your growth as a problem for **them**. If you did grow to your full potential, you're **not so easily** taken from or intimidated.

You're no longer a fly, you've become **the lion** … and from an Energy thief's perspective, this simply can't happen!

Energy Thieves are very clever at keeping their victims **small**. They'll use fear, intimidation and sometimes ply you with gifts.

Why?

Their life is easier when **your life** is easily influenced by

them.

The headspace of 'Kill it before it grows' is used.

Energy Thieves **know** that if you outgrew them, you'd see them for what they really are: small, inadequate and **totally** dependent.

Just remember, however strong they appear, their potential **is limited.**

Yours isn't.

You'll only need to outgrow them once.

What a lovely day that will be?

Walking past that Venus flytrap, this time as the lion!

Secondly, if you became everything you're supposed to, then **this world** (and the people in it) would have to **change**.

Change **is** needed but **highly** resisted.

Often by people who need it the **most**.

This is why most people start their journey of self-empowerment, but then stop; because of all the **unexpected resistance** they faced!

Now that you **expect it**, you can make appropriate **countermeasures**.

When it does happen; I want you to be able to say, 'The fact that it's happening, tells me I'm **on track**.'

Unfortunately, most people aren't prepared. No one tells you about the dark side.

After an encounter with an Energy Thief, they say, 'I've been hurt and I don't want it to happen again. So I'm going to protect myself.'

As a graphic illustration to the students, I get the sapling tree and put a big metal bucket over it to show how 'protecting yourself' works. I then ask the students, 'What's going to happen now?'

They answer, 'It won't grow.' Or, 'It will die slowly.'

Pausing for a second I ask,

'Was this tree born to hide …?

Were YOU born to hide?

If we take the bucket off, the plant can grow; but there's **the risk** of being hurt again,'

Know that with 'risk' comes **reward**.

Risk gives you the opportunity to outgrow and overcome.

Hiding has less risk, but it's a **guaranteed** slow death.

This is where you will need the most important factor in your growth, it begins with an '**R**' …

Resilience

What resilience can do for you is more important than your intellect or strength. Just because things are hard and it's hurting, **doesn't** mean you're going in the wrong direction!

It doesn't mean you should give up.

In fact, quite the **opposite**.

Know now that anything you **gave up** in your initial stage of growth,(and there will be a cost) you will get back ten fold. Better friendships, better support etc. The things that were **once hard** are now done **easily**.

Why?

All the **resistance** you faced wasn't there to stop you; It was there to make you **stronger**.

Resilience is **knowing** that the tough/dark times are there to make you **destiny ready**!

Awesome right!?

However, for this to *actually happen*, (and not just be a nice concept in your head) you need to know a magic number.

100%.

You need to commit yourself 100% to your **own growth**.

Nothing is gained if you're **half-hearted** about **your own empowerment**.

No one will do these actions for you and you can't wait for approval.

These are the actions unique to you. Actions that create an abundance of **good energy** for you. Things like happiness, social connection and a good night's sleep are only indicators of abundance, they aren't actions. Happiness, social connection and a good night's sleep come as a **result** of actions, (your actions) and they are found in the strangest of places.

For myself personally, I found them (Happiness, love,

peace,
etc) in No rules fighting. The fights were aggressive, fierce and
bloody, sometimes very bloody, but afterwards I met new friends. I had peace from training so hard and joy from applying myself to something I was so passionate about.

Other people couldn't see my reasoning. Even people close to me thought it was a waste of time (and didn't approve) because they didn't understand or share my passion.

So, when you first start your journey, **don't expect** to be **understood** or for others to **share your passion**.

You're **seeing** and **feeling** something **no one else can**.

Others will see it eventually, once you build it up; but **you** need to see it **first**. So start observing your own actions and what happens as a result of them.

Let me stress the 100% number. If you give 80% you get 80% back, 90% then 90% back, 99% then 99% back; However, if you commit 100% the **magic happens**, you get 1000% back, plus more!

Just on that, potentially you could already know, or currently be doing the **right** actions for yourself. However, because you're just not 100% committed to them, you're depriving yourself of the abundance those actions could give you.

Fighting made it easier for me to commit 100%. I knew I'd be smashed if I didn't. However, this world makes it very hard to maintain high standards, because its own standards are completely unclear.

Most Sheeple are only holding themselves to a standard held by other Sheeple.

A real person knows that they spend more time with themselves, than they do with anyone else. So, start creating a work rate and decisions (within yourself) that are held to a standard that **you** would be **proud** of.

Whenever I was hurting I would think, 'I'm going to work as hard as I need to, to be proud of myself afterwards.' Some say, 'Pain is temporary, Pride is forever.'

When you immerse yourself in your own development (truly **100%** committed), something amazing happens ...

Suddenly the resistance from others disappears!

Others see (or soon discover) there's nothing stopping you.

Soon as they see **that**, they leave you alone.

You know you've hit 100% when all the other things in your life, start lining up the way they should!

Why?

You finally have your actions, in line with your intentions.

Dreams become goals.

Goals become achievable.

Soon your reaching your goals because you're 100% committed.

If you're unsure exactly what to do in stage one, start by daily energising your body and getting quality rest. Find a physical discipline that you '**click with**' and do it **regularly**. I created the **Breathwork in Bed app** for this very reason, for people to discover better performance through better rest... and do it EASILY. *For more resources www.breathworkinbed.com.au

Exercise/rest is like water for your mind garden.

Things grow faster with **regular** watering.

That's why **regular** exercise is so important. It allows you to observe what **grows** in your mind garden. This is one-way people use to find their destiny.'

That's just part of the talk I give to high school students. I could write another book about exercising! However, just know the **most** important thing about exercise (besides consulting your Doctor beforehand) is not how hard you do it, but how **regularly** it's done.

It's obvious, but it needs to be said; You can do something that is comfortable and satisfying a lot longer than something that is uncomfortable and unsatisfying.

Make this your exercise code.

1000 workouts at 60%, **is better** than 10 workouts at 100%. For the first few months of exercising take it really easy. Something I'd tell my new clients is, 'Think of what you'd like to do. Then cut it in half, and take 20% off. Your goal in the first few months is to leave your workout with the feeling like you could've done more.' I know this sounds contradictory to my previous statement about giving 100%. However, there is a bigger picture that needs to be engaged.

What a lot of people don't realise is the hardest thing about exercise, isn't exercising! It's **organising** everything in your life so you can **turn up** to it. For this to happen, you need to make exercise a **priority**.

In a busy world, it's hard to make a priority of anything that is 'uncomfortable and unsatisfying.' Here's what happens if your exercise is uncomfortable or unsatisfying. At the very thought of exercise, unconsciously your mind will foresee pain and then tense your body up. Then, your mind will often find a legitimate excuse for you to avoid this discomfort.

Every wondered why just **before** exercise, all the excuses (and negative self-talk) rises to the surface? Our own head has 'Energy Vampires'. Negative parts of us that fight for their share of your energy. These parts are self-aware! They know that if you exercise, you'll become empowered and the balance of power will shift away from them. They scream the loudest just **before** it happens. They know they can't co-exist with true empowerment. Physical empowerment (done right), displaces them.

These days when I hear my own negative self-talk, (and it's always there just before exercise) I do two things;

First up, I see the negative talk for what it really is. 'I'm tired, let's just do this tomorrow' are just my disempowered parts saying, 'If you do this, we will die!' That's a good message to hear.

Secondly, I scan my body to find where the **tension** is. Once located (for me it's usually shoulders & neck) I then breathe deeply and relax them. Then in my mind, I smile and gently stare down the negative messenger; After all, it's a part of me, but I can't 'serve two masters'. That negative part of me needs to know **who's** making the decisions in my life ... and it's not them.

Alternatively, I 'Just Do It' and it goes away after 5-10 minutes.

Just remember that good energy has a shelf life of **24-36** hrs. Hence the importance of **regular** exercise. The energy in our mind and body needs regular gentle refreshment.

Interesting side note. Ever wondered why gyms these days are starting to look like nightclubs? Big audio and visual displays blasting your senses, overtly sexy (or belittling) marketing images everywhere, plus lots and LOTS of mirrors?

They're telling us (via evil subconscious suggestion), 'Everything that makes you, you, is seen in the mirror.' The evil part is how marketers convince us that our sense of self-worth is limited to only the **visible parts** of us. They effectively **block** your higher thinking and enslave you to the mirror (external influence).

WHY?

With all our modern conveniences, there's now no obvious reason to be physically fit. (Providing you're not a manual labourer or athlete.)

In this vacuum of reason to stay active, clever marketing

gives
you a reason by attacking your **self-worth**.

Marketers know that to Sheeple, *pain avoidance* will always beat their *higher thinking*.

This marketing induced '**Pain**' stops Sheeple out-thinking or outgrowing the flock or the mirror.

The reason most people don't exercise regularly isn't due to lack of proper facilities; it's due to the lack of proper reasons. Having the wrong reasons make it very hard to stay motivated.

To be physically empowered means understanding this;

Physical fitness isn't the goal.

Physical energy is.

Energy is a platform to your next stage of growth.

The Ancient Chinese had a saying, 'First the **body**, then the **mind**.'

Regardless of shape, you can be in an energised **state**.

The 'Energised State' allows your mind to flow naturally to your full potential; Also, to **outgrow** every obstacle in front of you. Our problems don't get smaller, we can become

bigger
than them.

Like I used to tell my clients with a smile, 'It will all **work out** if you just **work out**.'

Remember, your life is bigger than a billboard.

People see the stuff we're trying to hide, (even our reasons?!) So, don't just own it; Commit **100%** to **growing** it!

Take whatever time you need to outthink and **outgrow** the obstacles. They will come in many forms.

Speaking of obstacles ...

The SECOND FACE of the DARKSIDE

Unexpected resistance to your 'Self-empowerment' has **two sides**.

There's the resistance you face from **other people** (which we have just largely covered). Once you understand it, it's easy to see through and you'll only need to outgrow them once;

However, there is another area of resistance that isn't as easy to see past … even though it's obvious …

The resistance we face from **inside** ourselves.

It's a bit like a car. While it's going slow, there's no need to worry about wind resistance. As the car becomes more powerful and goes faster; anything that creates 'drag' becomes obvious.

In fact, '*High speed, low drag!*' became a saying in the Special Forces.

If we are to move forward, we need to be ready to get **rid** of (or find **healing** for) the things inside us that create drag and impede our top speed. Some people call this getting rid of the 'Dead Wood'.

Be ready for this, and know;

Everyone has **something** that needs to change, improve, heal or be gotten rid of.

Pain and aggravation are often **indicators** that something needs to change, improve, heal or be gotten rid of...

Some say, 'Life Sucks!' It sure would, if you're carrying heavy burdens on top of invisable karma.

Here's the **'game changer.'**

Emotional Pain and aggravation (in life) **is not** there to cause you pain and anger.

Pain and aggravation are simply messengers **knocking** at your door.

Pain and aggravation are trying to tell us that we need **to seek** healing.

Unfortunately, lifetimes and lives are lost (suicide) not understanding this.

Emotional injuries can be confusing because they aren't obvious (to the untrained eye); So I'll use a physical example to show my point.

Let's say I injured my arm, but I ignored it.

The pain would be a **messenger** telling me, 'Hey, this needs healing.'

I could **ignore** the messenger and just manage the symptoms; i.e., take pharmaceuticals or increase my personal pain threshold.

In fact, I could change my entire lifestyle to **avoid** any situation, or person that might aggravate the unhealed part of me.

As time passes, feelings of pain and aggravation would seem very **normal**. In fact, they start to become my guiding compass through life.

If I got angry, I'd blame others. 'They should know that's my sore spot! I've had it for so long.'

Unfortunately, in hanging onto my pain, I would cause pain to others. I'd hurt people close to me with my attitude of, 'If you can't tiptoe around my pain, then get lost.'

My pain threshold would become my badge of honour.

If someone with the same emotional problem sought help and got healing, I'd call them weak. The idea of my pain being **'fixable'** is an insult to all the pain I had tolerated up until that point.

(This is Crazy, but yet it happens all the time!?)

My avoidance tactics still wouldn't stop 'the messenger' (pain & aggravation) knocking on my door, or my productivity decreasing.

This is where we get it so wrong in the western world.

We ignore 'Holistic Healing'. We think we'll end up as one of those 'Alternate types' eating tofu, celery and not washing.

I worked with many injured ex-defence members who struggled with the concept of healing the **whole person**. They struggled because they were trained to **ignore** natural tendencies – that is, fear, pain, fatigue. In fact, how much fatigue and pain they could endure was a badge of honour for them. Asking for help was considered weakness. Of course, there is a time and place to harden up. This country was made great by such attitudes. However, if 'hardening up' becomes your only option, harder times are coming.

So I'd explain 'Holistic Healing' to them like this;

'If you saw me working out in the gym, would you call me weak? Of course not! I'm in the gym because I have a 'desire to be stronger'. It's that same 'desire to be stronger' that brings me to the Psychologist, the Yoga class, the men's group. I want **every part** of my life to get stronger, not just my **bench press**.'

'Holistic healing' doesn't just make us **better** people, it makes us more **productive** people. Unfortunately, for most westerners, seeing the 'Commercial Application' to 'Holistic Healing' is the **only way** they'll accept it.

'Holistic healing' must take place if we want to have an abundance in **every** area of our lives.

Our own internal blockages must be acknowledged and removed for us to reach our full potential. No question.

Just on that, there is good and bad news when seeking 'Holistic Healing.'

GOOD NEWS: when you find the **right** provider, it takes very little time to heal.

BAD NEWS: It can be **very hard** to find the right providers.

The problem is that these 'healing' places are like coffee shops. There's one on every corner! They advertise everywhere. Unfortunately, myself (and many others) have discovered that you have to work really hard to find one that's **right** for you. Also, good providers generally have long waiting lists.

Healing is easy, but finding the right 'healing environment' can take a lot of time. Which is a real problem. Most people (especially us blokes) don't ask for help until it's at **crisis stage**.

When a crisis happens, they often need to see someone right **now**. As a result, they'll take whoever is most available at the time. Which isn't always the best, or best suited for them.

Many times I heard people honestly say: *'I tried getting help and it didn't help. In fact, it made things worse!? So I'm never trying again.'*

I'd love to say all providers of healing are great! Unfortunately, the world is the way it is, and not the way we want it to be.

A person's academic achievements may sound very impressive and I'm sure they studied very hard. Unfortunately, high academic standards only get you in the room. They don't always create an effective healer.

FYI, academic achievements mean nothing to someone who is damaged, fatigued and in desperate need.

Good healers that have skill, motivation and **heart** to connect and energise those that are damaged and fatigued. Unfortunately, they are incredibly rare!

Personally, I tried many practitioners and had just as many **bitter** disappointments. Disappointments are a massive withdrawal on an account that's already overdrawn. Consequently, protecting what's left becomes your new game plan. Being fatigued and very suspicious of medical 'Specialists' is a dangerous mix. The closest I came to giving into violence (in a civilian setting) was after experiencing complete apathy and incompetence from medical specialists who I had turned to in my hour of need. The damage I could have done to myself and others **scared me**. After that, I could have easily avoided all medical specialists and lived a life in complete social isolation. However, it gave me real empathy for people seeking help.

It would've been soo much easier if someone had told me that the hard work isn't getting healed; it's finding the **right** healer. They're simply not all created equal. Hence the importance of this book.

Here's an example of my own personal timeline in search of healers.

3 years to find a good GP

4 years to find a good Psychiatrist

5 years to find a good Yoga instructor

6 years to find a good psychologist (this was by far the hardest search).

However, the six years of searching saved me 50 years of pain and probably multiple family breakdowns.

My favourite ancient Chinese saying is:

'Through strength, learn gentleness.

Through gentleness, learn true strength.'

Firstly, we must get strong. To get to our strongest, (and most gentle) we must also get healing.
Healing is the key to being **gentle** with others. Just ask the family of a person refusing to get help.

After all, how strong and gentle could I get if I ignored my injuries? Ever noticed how life has a way of hitting you at your weakest point?

Our own journey of healing has incredible value. In fact, sometimes the **most** valuable thing we can offer to others, is to share our **own** journey of healing with them.
If I hadn't gone through Afghanistan, PTSD, family breakdown, loosing all my money, pharmaceutical dependency and substance abuse; This book & Breathwork in Bed wouldn't have existed. I **certainly did not** see it at value to me. the time, but those experiences were adding **incredible**

Do you think there are other regular people 'out there' struggling with the same things you are?

Maybe all a person really needs, is to know another **'regular person'** who has successfully overcome a similar hurdle or challenge in life?

Maybe all they need, *is to know* **you** ...

6

THE POWER OF BEING A REGULAR PERSON

The power of being a regular person begins with the realization that there are *millions* of us. Just think about the magnitude of that for a moment …

Anything you're facing (or have faced) you can bet others have or are currently. Everything from failure to success, healing, body image, money issues, family, self-development, relationships, trouble sleeping, loss, fear, anger, you name it! It's powerful to know that if you find a way for yourself (in anything), you find a way for many, many others. You are not alone.

It became very evident to me (when I was about to die in Afghanistan) that all I needed was to **know** another regular person who had found a way forward. They didn't even have to be there with me; I just needed to 'know of them'.

There's power in this Knowledge.

The ANZACs who inspired me on that dark night were just regular people who didn't let their fear **control them**; they simply kept moving forward. Their simple actions were so powerful that they empowered me without them even being there! They empowered me, and they weren't even alive!? They reached out (beyond their own timeline) and gave me real-time, kick-ass empowerment!

Author ANZAC Day speech 2019. The 'ANZAC Spirit' (chapter 8).

Do you see the implications of this?

Wouldn't that mean that you and me, as regular people, could do the same for others in this life, and beyond?

Is this what immortality looks like?

This perspective changes everything.

When you as a regular person, make progress in your life. You become incredibly valuable to millions of others.

At some point in the future, other people are going to say to you, 'My mind had 'Impossiblised' my situation, but you showed me it's possible and that's **all** I needed.'

Personally, I like to imagine millions of people (I haven't met yet and may never meet in my life time) 'willing me on' because the progress I make (in my regular life) shows others that;

Firstly, it's actually possible.

Secondly, I have accessible options to share.

More options = more hope.

It may take a lot of time to achieve something in your life. A month, a year or ten years; however, this is the time you'll be saving others and they'll be very glad you did.

My own journey of recovery showed me the power of regular people. As a war veteran, I didn't know (or wouldn't admit to) having PTSD and depression. Unfortunately, ignoring your mental health doesn't stop it affecting you or your **family**.

My journey of healing could have taken **much** longer if not for one single (very special) conversation.

This conversation wasn't with a doctor or professional psychologist, but with a humble and honest Vietnam Veteran.

It pays to note that soldiers (like a lot of blokes) have a big problem asking for help. The story we tell ourselves is, 'If you ask for 'help' that means you're 'weak'. If you're weak, you let the team down … and I'll die before I let the team down.'

There's **a lot** of defence members (and fellow humans) suffering without admitting there is a problem.

In Australia, we have lost more than twice as many soldiers to suicide than to bullets in Afghanistan.

I was headed the same way.

That is, until this one conversation with an honest Vietnam Veteran. He 'lost it' in front of me. Through anguished tears, he said, 'Why was I hanging onto this for soo long? Who was I trying to impress? What was I trying to prove? What would my life be like if I started getting help 35 years and three marriages ago??'

I was at a loss … After gathering myself, I said, 'I can't turn back the clock, but if it means anything, you've made me want to start my journey of healing now. So thank you. I hope you know that you just saved me 35 years. Know your time wasn't spent in vain. If I can, I will be doing the same for others.'

The Vietnam Veteran give me this look I'll never forget; it was like he got, closure …

Soon after that encounter, I started working with the not-for-profit group Mates4Mates. It's a charity that helps current and ex-serving members of the Australian defence force who are wounded, injured or ill, recover from their service (and their families). Working at Mates4Mates I personally created powerful programs that helped (and continue to help) a great many current and ex-serving members. The most powerful part of any program are the conversations that are had during it.

Nearly every week a member would approach me saying, 'If it wasn't for that conversation we had here at Mates4Mates, I would've killed myself.'

I worked there for several years …

Every time someone said that to me, I would think back to that Vietnam Veteran who had helped me, and I'd quietly thank **him**.

His actions aren't written down in the history books (besides this one). He was only a regular guy and the conversation lasted about 20 minutes. However, for myself, my loved ones and the many I helped at Mates4Mates (and continue to help), the effects of that 20 minute conversation will ripple for lifetimes to come ….

This example gives us perspective, or what I like to call the 'Empowered perspective'.

Empowered Perspective tells us an amazing fact;

To benefit the world we live in; all we need to be is **ourselves**.

However, it must be our **Empowered Selves**.

We already have the raw capital - our names and a heartbeat. All we need is the right self-investment.

Interesting point, I actually disagree with the saying, 'Everyone is Special.' Yes, we need to treat everyone equally, but we are all born differently. Saying, **'I'm special'** and leaving it at that is a bit like saying, 'I have a dollar in the bank' then expecting to become wealthy.

Everyone does naturally have value and energy in varying amounts. However, seeing your **own** can be hard. After all, our consumer society keeps telling us that for our value to be real, it must be seen (and commented on) by others. It's an invisible rule that unfortunately enslaves the potential of all Sheeple. It's very rare to have someone ask themselves, 'What value do I have, that only I can see?' Then consequently ask, 'How can I develop it?'

It is crucial that we see our own value, with our own eyes. Otherwise, our self-worth will only be measured through the eyes of others. That is very unstable base to build on.

Should our self-worth be relative to what others think? Should our value and energy be limited by the limitations of others?

Personally, I've noticed people frequently project their own limitations, (their own sense of what's possible) onto others. When I applied to join the Commandos at the age of 30. I was the oldest person attempting it. Everyone said, 'You're too old!' That discouraged me. Until I realised they weren't saying, 'You can't do it.' They were actually saying, '**I can't** do it.' They weren't talking about me, they were talking about themselves. They just assumed **their** limitations were **mine**. That was a breakthrough moment for me! Although, it didn't stop the younger recruits giving me the nickname, 'Old Man Tommo'.

Should we worry if other people believe in us or not?

Seeing is believing.

After you're successful, you'll hear, 'I always knew you could do it.'

'Actually,' I'd think, 'That's the opposite of what you said initially.'

Be gentle with others but remember, only 'you' change 'you'.

7
IN CLOSING

If someone was to ask me a deep question like, 'What's our reason for being here?' My answer would be, 'Our purpose in this world is to create an abundance. To live abundantly, and not sweat the small stuff. Namely, travel your own unique path to your own unique abundance ... Then show others how to do it in far **less** time.'

Our own journey will show us what we need to **change or improve** within ourselves. Prepare yourself now and be ready to spend the energy needed for self-repair. It's going to happen and often it will be a very valuable thing you can share with others.

Just remember, good energy has a shelf life of about 24-36 hours. It needs to be refreshed daily or you risk being two different people in the same body. The lion needs to be unlocked by a daily physical or spiritual investment, or you risk being the fly.

Daily self-investment will give you a renewable energy source. Knowing you can renew your energy creates real confidence that no one can take.

Strength and success are no longer 'maybes', they're just a matter of time. However, just remember that true strength/success is for service, not status.

What we do for ourselves, we eventually want **others**, to be able to do for **themselves**, also.

Be selfishly wise. Have boundaries, but also have space for fellow humans. We are creating More for More; not just 'More

for Me.'

The world's Trillion-dollar trade on temporary solutions to me, highlights the incredible vacuum for **real** options and **real**

energy. Consequently, if you create an abundance in

yourself,
and help others do the same; you become a very valuable commodity.

This book has shown you how to develop 'that something' *inside* of you; the something that could change everything *outside* of you.

It all starts here with you putting the book down and asking yourself, 'What value do I see in me?' Then, 'What's one thing I could do, to create an abundance of that?'

8

THE ANZAC SPIRIT

I've added this chapter, 'The ANZAC Spirit', here. It is a talk I gave on ANZAC Day (25 April) in 2019. It is another way of looking at the experiences and insights I've talked about in the other parts of this book, and it also adds something special. Tim.

*

On ANZAC Day, it is customary to talk of wars, of battles won and lost. After all, War has a very interesting mix of fear and courage. Today however, I want to talk about the fear and courage, in healing.

For all wars must end in healing. The healing of broken bodies, the healing of broken minds, and the healing of broken hearts. This is how a nation heals.

The importance of supporting those, who support the troops when they come home, cannot be understated. Transitioning out of the defence force and into civilian life can be a unseen battle ground claiming many silent ADF (Australian Defence Force) casualties.

There is fear in battle, but there's also fear in admitting you have a problem and you need healing.

My name is Tim Thomas, I served with the Australian Special forces Commandos with deployments to East Timor and Afghanistan.

On ANZAC day, we remember that 104 years ago the ANZAC's formed up to capture the Gallipoli peninsula in an attempt to open up the Dardanelles to the allied naval fleet. The objective was to capture Constantinople, now called Istanbul in Turkey.

*

The ANZAC's landed on Gallipoli and met fierce resistance from the Ottoman Turkish defenders. Their plan to knock Turkey out of the war quickly became a stalemate, and the campaign dragged on for eight long months.

At the end of 1915, the allied forces were evacuated. Both sides suffered heavy casualties and endured great hardships. Over 8,000 Australian soldiers were killed. News of the landing on Gallipoli had a profound impact on Australians at home. The 25th of April became the day on which Australians remember the sacrifice of those who had died in the war.

*

History is full of war and battles. However, today we mark what makes ANZAC day so significant. So significant that we even talk about the ANZAC Spirit. That's unique. Not many battles in all of history have a SPIRIT attached to them.

Let me ask you, are the ANZAC's important to you? 'Is ANZAC spirit still important and relevant in modern Australia?'

After all 104 years is a very long time!

We use the words 'Lest we forget', but what exactly should we be remembering?

Ladies and gentlemen, I want to give you something very special. Something the ANZACS personally gave me. My wish is that what the ANZACs gave me, will powerfully, positively and permanently impact your lives, just like it did mine.

Australian troops were part of the Gallipoli peninsula campaign that occurred in 1915, skip forward 94 years to 2009. Australian Troops are now deployed to Afghanistan as part of Operation Slipper. I was part of Bravo Company in the Australian Special Forces Commandos. We would seek out and engage with an Enemy that was very intelligent, and we were on their home ground.

This home ground advantage was used to great effect in the mountainous terrain of Afghanistan. A reminder of this fact, to those of us on the ground, were the destroyed Russian tanks scattered everywhere.

As Australians, we used the BUSH MASTER. A heavily armoured vehicle that would protect the soldiers inside. As special forces, we had a select few Bush Masters, however most of us travelled in light skin vehicles.

Picture a 4wd with the roof cut off and machine guns fixed in place. If you go to the Australian War Museum in Canberra, there is one on display there.

We were doing operations outside the wire. On this one night, deep in enemy territory, we received intel telling us that there was a RPG (Rocket Propelled Grenade) ambush waiting for us ahead. This wasn't unusual, but the mountainous terrain didn't allow our convoy to take any other path, and our enemy knew that. We had to go forward with our enemy waiting for us.

So the order came down to put all the heavily armoured BUSH MASTERS (that RPGs couldn't penetrate) to the rear of the convoy. Tactically, the rear vehicle is least defended and so it's the one that usually gets attacked.

Remember, our vehicle had no armour. It was simply a 4WD with no roof.

However, in the confusion and rush before the ambush, we got cut off and ended up as the rear vehicle in the convoy …

Everyone in that vehicle knew what was going to happen next.

There was the vehicle commander Al; driving was Upai and myself on the 50cal machine gun. As 'Al' got his machine gun ready he said, 'Fella's, if this goes the way I think it will, it's been a absolute honour serving with you …'

It's funny, but in moments like that you notice the small things. Like hearing your own 'Dinky Di' Australian accent spoken back to you, in a very foreign land. However, this was not a movie, and we didn't have a pause button …

I'd done a few 'Ramp ceremonies' before, where the flag covered bodies of Australian soldiers were returned home. Some of the fallen were closer to me than brothers. I remember thinking before the ambush, (and this is where soldiers use black humour) 'They're going to return our flag- covered bodies to Australia. They're going to carry us down the ramp of the aeroplane with all this BS ceremony, all because we got cut off in traffic!?!'

Joking aside, extreme fear and anger began shutting my whole body down.

You'd think that as a soldier I'd get used to fear. Fact was I never did, but there's something helpful about being exposed to fear so often. You do get a very clear understanding of how fear actually works, and it's fascinating!

I found that Fear has a goal, and it's not to scare you.

Fear's ultimate goal is to immobilise you. To stop you from even trying. Your head might say, 'I know I should be doing this ...' but fear stops your body from even attempting it.
Once you understand that, you realise that you don't overcome fear with love.

You overcome fear, with ACTION.

Taking ACTION dispels FEAR.

Conversely, in-action, not doing what you know you should, grows it.

I then took a course of action that has sculpted the rest of my life.

I said to myself, 'Tim, do you know anyone who has done this before? How did they get through it?!'

Fact was that I didn't know anyone … Australia seemed so far away. The night somehow got darker, and I began to feel very alone.

Until I began to think 'outside' my own timeline. I realised then that I did know some men who had done exactly this. I knew that on a night as dark as this, the original ANZACs came face-to-face with a foe that was waiting for them on their home ground.

What did the ANZACs do? They kept moving forward without letting their fear control them. They kept moving forward without letting their fear control them! Despite hardships, despite a bad situation, despite an enemy intent on killing them.

The outside world could not stop them, from seeing the power inside them.

We often say, 'Lest we forget ...' But it was like those ANZAC diggers were poking me in the chest saying, 'Lest YOU forget!' 'Lest you forget the power inside you! Lest you forget the power of looking after your mates!'

Even though the beach landing was almost 100 years ago, and their stories are told through history books, the ANZACs were right there with me in that moment, and I was no longer alone!

It was like the sun coming up at midnight.

My whole body felt illuminated!

The ANZAC's 'actions' of 1915 dispelled my 'fear' in 2009.

My actions, then became fearless. I could act and think without fear.

Before I hit the ambush, I thought, 'They might find my body in a few minutes time, but you know what they're not going to find? Bullets! All of my bullets are getting used, and you know what!? If I survive this, all of my dreams, are getting lived!'

I got through that night by discovering the ANZAC spirit.

I got through the rest of my Afghan deployment and can enjoy days like this because of the ANZAC spirit.

Unfortunately, for many defence personnel it can take a long time to enjoy days like this. It certainly did for me.

It took me even longer to figure out why I survived when men far better than me died.

However, that's part of the healing that must follow war. This can take time, as there is much fear and courage in seeking healing.

Fear of admitting there is a problem, the courage to let it go, and live life differently.

This is true for everyone, not just soldiers.

Part of my healing journey, and I see it as part of the reason I survived, is to revive the ANZAC spirit in this country. To people like you and me.

It's important to note that the ANZAC's who inspired me on that dark night were just regular people, as regular as anyone. The big difference was, they didn't let their fear control them.

Can you see the implications of this?

Can you see the example the ANZACs have shown us?

They're trying to show us that, you and me, as regular people, could do the same for others, in our lifetime, and beyond!
In our life, and in this modern world 100 plus years later, there are all sorts of knowledge a person can attain. However, imagine this; what if all a person needed to know, to be fearless, successful and find healing, was to know someone who had done it before?

What if all that person needed to know … was You?

Can you feel the ANZACs poking you in the chest saying, 'Lest you forget that!'

Ladies and gentlemen, welcome to the ANZAC Spirit.

ANZAC day is once a year, but the ANZAC Spirit is for everyday of the year.

It's now our time to follow their example. To take action, and dispel our fear. Despite hardships, despite bad situations, despite any opposition intent on stopping us.

It's now our time to finish the story.

That is why the ANZAC spirit needs to be protected, maintained, and cherished, and handed down to our children as a very important part of what it means to be Australian.
The ANZAC spirit changed everything for me. My sincere wish is that it does the same for you.

Lest we forget …

Written and Spoken by Tim Thomas, ANZAC Day 2019 Greenslopes Private Hospital, Brisbane, Queensland, Australia.

The video of this talk can be found at
https://youtu.be/69XD8mFhis4

AFTERWORD

I sincerely hope you enjoyed this book. To me there is no higher calling than to heal oneself & give your gifts generously to the world ie Helping others to do what you did, in far less time. To that end, share this book with those who you think would benefit. Your own journey will be assisted when you surround yourself with people who want to **grow with you**.

It's important to remember that positive change is made permanent only with **repetition**. Install the Breathwork in Bed app on your phone if you haven't already. *Planned launch is December 2023. Please join out mailing list for updates on product releases www.breathworkinbed.com.au

I encourage you to re-read or re-listen to sections of this book that were of most benefit to you. I guarantee you'll get something new every time you do. I **always** do.
For further resources or updates please visit us online;
www.breathworkinbed.com.au;
Instagram: breathworkinbed
TikTok: breathworkinbed
Face Book: breathworkinbed

REFERENCES

i http://www.cnbc.com/id/100957882 ... Globally $435 billion is spent on illegal drugs ...

ii https://www.mordorintelligence.com/industry-reports/energy-drinks-market ... Caffeinated Energy drinks ...

iii http://en.wikipedia.org/wiki/Economics_of_coffee ... over 2250,000,000 cups of coffee consumed globally every day ...

Printed in Australia
Ingram Content Group Australia Pty Ltd
AUHW011147130923
383625AU00003B/3